Hearts

&

Highways

Chris Noonan

To My Grandparents,

Thank you for showing me which of life's roads to travel.

With love and gratitude.

- CJN -

Hearts & Highways

Courage to carry
Winter's deep water purity,
      cleansing the pores of those that
we seek.

To journey there
      And back again,
A million soft footsteps
      And the beauty of the pen.

Lost in worlds unremembered,
      Seeking to identify with ancestral
cultures
Amidst the scanning paths
      Of neurological vultures.

The sweet release
      Of my hidden ode,
Given to you,
      Kept in time,
For the young and the old.

When we look where we've been,
　　　Do we see where we go?
The lonely song
　　　From eyes so old.
And we move forward
　　　As each day does pass,
Wishing away our futures
　　　Under time's long looking glass.

Walking the road is never as hard
　　　As walking alone,
Time marches along
　　　A highway of hearts calling you
home.

Arrows blazing, soaring through air,
Please let me see the blinking faces of the
freshly awakened.

Long past and still unsolved,
Storm-fronts refresh, a sweet resolve
of life's long quest.

Friends and lovers and stories rolling
rhyme,
Released from the bow
To free you from time.

Repent.
Is all I can muster in riddled truths
Of the mysterious jester,
Holding an hour
Of pelting rain,
To steam or simmer
Seems all the same.

Covered in tar,
Earth's melting core,
Moaning beside mountains,
Crawling the hardwood floor.
Reaching for blindness,
Will you open my door?

Eco-feminists rummaging through post-
Napoleonic Moscow, dreams made
material, survivors of thoughts incubation,
craftsmanship's manifestation. Dazzling
brave-hearts masking appeal and shipping
culture East. One building amidst the
many, carved in indigo paints and ruby
reds, a testament to the time when Tsars
led.

Now France freezes and Moscow's ahead.

Leading proudly with disco night shock,
curling bodies delight in symmetries
bright electro-revolution, underground
spinners luminescent as psychedelic liquid
dancers. Repeating patterns and laser
light enhancers, pink hair display, rioting
for attention the piercings promenade, the
unwinding path of statement and refusal,
vibrating echolocation of 23rd century
techno-crazed sensation.

Identities clash in techno time flash fad,
Be anyone, a form from beyond, a
conveyance of unfamiliar recognition.
Two selves merged in planetary
atmospheric gases, wobbling in
inconsistencies and festive costumes.
Mark the night with your privilege,
Life and self; transparent and camouflage.

Stars and fields
And bright molten metal,
Clashing configurations
Of the company prowl.

The beast assumed, stood in mute awe,
There was no howl in death's rhythmic
arrival.

A reawakening, a deep space exhalation,
Distance measured with arcane devices
And passed through channels of sub-
conscious recollection.

Sojourner meets mountains of Mars,
To look back at zealous Roman czars.
Pieces of your past unravel,
Reaching toward new hope of the judge's
hard gavel.

Looking back,
Tracing footprints for the cycles justified
end,
So new life's we create
In time's soft circles spiral.

Madness for a minute
In life's changing course,
Redemptive acts pressing
Perspective's kind force.

~ Lead me once
        And I may follow,
    Guide me tonight
        And I'll be there tomorrow~

Listen softly
     And you shall hear
A thousand brave drums
     Announcing a year.

Recording our past
     In digitized form/
Connecting our futures,
     So far from the norm.

Mortars and planes
     In a picture above,
     Posters of futures wired with love.

Scripted passages of a new turn,
Another night passes in slow amber
Autumn,
Calculating days into seconds
For a chance to catch a passing ship.

Landing in provinces of rich sultry
meadow,
Finding a map to coordinates beyond,
Looking for something gypsy fortunes
foretold.

The coming of angels in the break of day,
The dancing of saints
Amongst the cats vicious play.

Amid uncertain hours, forgotten wilted
flowers.
Gripping to calls in the unseen distance,
A protest for freedoms-
Sealed with weapon's blind insistence.

Soon summer soldiers put down their
guns,
Transporting time and a message that we
won.

Seeking old beats of forgotten nights,
Sirens reach for
the child's cold, wet feet.

Embrace gentle rays
Of steady cosmic course,
Halos from heaven's sweet coded verse.

Rippling futures-
The remembered and the lost.
Gathering dust and trying to flee,
Locked inside,
With nothing more to see.

One has said to think
Is to be;
And I may see this truth and clarity
for you and me,
Of the beast and of the free,
But if all were to act as they think,
Would they be caged
Or suddenly assuaged?

So many verses recorded in time,
Capturing our life's simple crime.
The crime stands so obvious
But difficult to confine,
It's a simple notion
Of being trapped in a mind.

But fortune is happy
And the mind is such endearing refuge,
Burning with the desires of the western
inferno.
This prison is perfect,
Its warden does surely know,
For release it; and there's no telling where
it would go.

Clocks counting
Slow time commute,
Challenging our lifetimes
Diligent debut.

Gathering the pieces
Of a new day's delight,
Laughing sobriety
Echoing through the night.

Trains in motion
And steady seasoned thought commotion.
Calcite relics wash ashore
A photo of celestial being
To forever adore.

Endearing muse
Of color blind eye,
Laughing vacancies
From another seasons dreaded rhyme.
Fixing a spot in the road up ahead,
Waiting for nothing,
I already bled.

Bugs clinging to desperate
Decay of the log's rotting wood.
Shedding a life and passing
Through channels, brief moments
Of steady recollection.

Rot as you should
Fallen log of the old forest floor.
Rot and be merry in your decay,
Remembering the soil's way:
Through the grass and destined
For clay.

My memories haunt me
Like an unfed ghost,
I ran to confess
But never spoke,
I thought it was a dream
But never awoke,
I stepped out of line
And hung for my crime.

Long days and nights
Sharp like cut gems
Mingling on a stranger's
Dangling diadem.

Handcuffed and restrained
Practiced magic,
Where death and life
Are the same.

Then to feel angry winds
push riddling thoughts
Of half spun fantasy.

Thin glaciers of time warped perception.
In your aged youth is beauty
And the sweet birth
of the shedding skin
of lives you've already lived.

Tears in time and slow progression:

Marching solemnly in military procession.

Cold nights of a dog's war,
Fought with honor and mythical folklore.

Healing slowly the wounds from before,
We'll get there again in pages of passion,
We'll reach a new forest and learn a new
lesson.

In seasons of somber steady bird's delight,
I love you forever my guiding moonlight.

Ravenous knowledge thirst,
Scavenger nights, lonely and wild,
Active knowledge hurts
Tabula rasa, innocent child.

Prevented from passing, as time marches
on,
Traveling mind to mind,
Confined and undefined,
Passing strangers puzzle piece glance,
Chance's mirage for our summer dance.
Blinded by cave's shapeless shadow echo
& alone on the shore, ready to know.

Passion's page has struck us like
Tower clock pendulum persistence.

Training for life in off-hours
Cold as winter's incarnation,
renewal refreshes and imbues
a steady saintly sensation.

Sages come to bring their magnanimity,
The suffering of many in blinding heat's
intensity.

Once I felt you;
At edge's extreme - looking for more,
I seek your face, all others I ignore.

A caged bird flew,
The air stings like morning dew.
Lost in scribbled lines of thought,
Dreaming of century's
Swirling sun spot.

Careful of the heights you meet:
Your wings are wax
And melt in the heat.

You've been away for a year
Or more,
Each day passes,
Memories
Harder to ignore,
I've seen your life
In a scattered flash,
I dreamt of your face as
A million others seemed to pass.

I closed my eyes
And there she was,
Through a thousand years she traveled
To make I us.

We embraced under musical skies
And danced to the break of dawn,
She taught me new footsteps to love's
Oldest songs.

Two lovers swam in the sea,
Laughing and loving
In paradise's eternity.

The city worker meets his end.
A cycle of clocks,
Laboring all day
In electric industrial shock.

Break him from this mold
Of conformity,
Show him travel, destitution and
immunity.

Responsible to the day and nothing more.

A life of wondering
Interrupts slavery's whore.

Iron truss,
Bold, strong,
Repelling implosion
To the faithful's delight.
Cruciform, forged in fire,
Molten made metal;
Survivor of sunken pits
Of zero ground wreckage.

Imbued with dull balmy orange,
Time tempting mineral decay.
Many year's past
Solid crosshairs stay,
Reassuring the broken,
Confirming the ascent
In colliding time when
Man and his maker
Question the made.

Scattered dots
Growing bright,
Diffusing molecules
Spectral light.
Feelings in the breeze
Bring you to your knees,
Lead me to palaces
Of laughter and the
Kingdom of love,
Please.

A new tale is told
From a season of old.

Indians, long wooden crafts,
The river runs long and wide
To you, this I will confide.

Ancestral beats calling to protect
The tribe,
Our mirrored customs
Till the end of time, or for a bribe?

Waters do carry currents
Marked signs of Earth lament.
Brave and bold
Trampled and burned
For precious gold,
Teach and trade,
Ancient laws
Never fade.

Crawling reptile,
Precious metal.
Bound by your way
Built of your clay,
Priests in robes
Preaching about days of old.

When God and man mingled
And cataclysms signaled:
The beginning begun,
The end is won,
The way is paved,
The faithful saved.

Late night sunlight
And trees gentle breeze,
Ten thousand soldiers
Fighting to be free,
A thousand brave
Sailors traversing the sea.

Sailing for his majesty
And battling over a tax
On tea.

We fought bravely,
Jesus save me.
Splintered like wood,
This can't be good.

Ten thousand men,
Persuasive pen,
Guide this boat
All that he wrote.

If you want to win,
Stay free from sin.
Put down your sword
And follow the Lord.

Darkness came upon us like a black cloak,
Choking, grasping for air,
Look to the heavens
Who dares to care?
Up in the highest heights,
Seven candles burned through
The night.
Brunt offerings/
Slaughtered beasts
For allotment above,
So many have past
In the dark shadows
Of night, I crawled
Across your floor once more
In petrified remembrance.

Fires burning slowly in the mirror's
image.
A million unheard voices gathered
For a night of dancing.

The feast lasts several days,
Girls sang and got wild on wine.

In the depths of pale winter
Celebrations marked
Rituals for village's
Seasoned rites of passage.

Twin pinstripes,
Dark mysterious hats
Tilted slightly across young handsome
faces.

Black sweet luxury cars pull to the curb,
Tinted windows lowered and money
exchanges.

Looking toward new years,
I saw distant glimpses of 18th century
frosted twilights.

We shuddered, reflecting on our journey.
A footstep in time's rushing rivers, closer
toward an end, further from the known.
Linear passage does not comprehend.

It's been hundreds of years or maybe
more since I've seen your pleasant ways.

While emancipating your egg-nest,
I pondered the margin's of the blessed
And persuaded the field clearers to
confess.

They replied, "blind, broken and
breathing, we look for these nights
to heal and protect. To encourage and
move forward to look back and reflect."

A day, a time, a lesson I cannot forget.
The junction of the past we met,
Never look back with both eyes and never
let go,
Stay to your course and watch how you
grow.
So thank you for teaching me so well
Presently reunited, with so much to tell.

Autumn twilight near
Hope, danger and despair
A round wreath of laurels lay
Upon a memory brave as day
Rallied at crossroads common
Bargains, compromises and duty's
summon
Into the night trepid and tall
We fight only against the fall
And at the final roll call
Of the blessed souls remembered
We stand and say we never surrendered.

On the far distant hills
I stretch to hear your breath.

Your words of wisdom
In times of strife.
Your calm resolution
Guiding my life.

Amazed at your love
And sweet tenderness,
Humbled by your example
And gentle kindness.

(For Mom)

Dragons stalk the forest night, hope is
ablaze, hope is ablaze, hotter than breath.
Dark foreboding eyes, full of
remembrance and depth. Gentle, careful,
purposeful footsteps plot their journey,
marked and led by a dim and distant scent.
Tree boughs bend to the ones who travel
by fallen moonlight, the chaulky glow that
counts our days, contrasted to the northern
star cousin that orients our pilgrimage.
We have chosen this way, better than our
silent, absent alternative. They are close
at heart always, this small brave band,
tracking St. George to tell him that we are
no monsters.

Distorted agonizing
Journey, carrying me far from palaces of
slight comfort.

Dragged by your lawmen
To the frozen dungeon of unspoken times.

Trapped by ill fate
I struggled all my life
And sit mesmerized by the
Slow absent cruelty of your punishment.

They told me the madcap laughed
But I never heard him,
It was a summer day
Not too long ago
I strained to hear
But there was not even an echo.
And so I retrace my footsteps
And retreat to my dwelling.
If you hear of him please let me know,
If he laughs please tell me so.
I have chased many wild thoughts
To the distant edge
But it is in the shrill enjoyment
Of the madcap's laughter
That I seek and continue
To chase after.

(For Syd Barrett, 1947 - 2006)

I sent the poor men to the long soup line,
The humble church selflessly doling out a
warm
Meal.

I saw the lost ones struggling
For necessities and heard
Others gasp in astonishment
At life's harshest truths.

Wonderers of an innocent age congregate
At the ancient home.

There is no fee and seating is limited.
Love is too for these strange nomads
fighting free.

Melting ice of winter's
Silent withdrawal.
Creeping in caverns
Searching remnants
Of life's earliest arrival.

We gather to collect the fragments
Of yesterdays slow thought circle.

Encrypted messages
Speak again,
A promise of love
And life without end.

Stars are the eyes
From those who've past,
Searching the Earth
For dreams that will last.

The wind is the breath
From those who are gone,
Whispering comfort
For a heart that is long.

The sun is the smile
From an old friend
And the gentle assurance
That we'll meet again.

In the fourth year
We learned how to fly.
Brilliant feathers grew
On shoulders cold as stones.

Warm wings replaced
Old meek bones.
We aspired great
Heights where the angels dance
And assembled glowing
Sacrifices selected by chance.

Alone on the mountain
Man meets his
Silent steady maker.

Each, one by one,
Seek to see
Behind the sun,
All of us will have our
Turn,
To stand in line
Only to learn,
Love is the action that will get you
through,
Many are called, but the chosen are few.

Midnight dreams
So kind it seems
To look deep in heavens far star scene.
Wondering rovers sent to Mars,
Two strangers meet,
Post-atmospheric heat,
Stories exchanged
And happiness retained.

So distant you seem
Controlling from your command room
sitting,
Constructing a framework for an end that
is fitting,
Minds, machines and bright space dreams.

Seven cycles wind to their finale
In the birth of accomplishment.

That night the beat
Came from afar, unannounced, a distant
realm
Of being, confusion
Followed.

Strange composures of your sound fresh
and bold as the awakened dead.

Cool as the midnight moon
And illustrious as a king and throne.

Their we sit watching the vibrations of
your serenade,
Full of praise and awe we sat amazed.

Many will come to revision your toned
original
Construction;
Many will embrace the steady course of
structure
And bow to the thrill of the seeing the
parade of souls for the first time.

I love you.
No other words
Can be so true.

I hold your hand
And hope you understand.

No one competes,
There is no there other
I will call my lover.

While looking for God,
I noticed He found me.

She is the heroine of all my fantasy,
The keeper of all my dreams.
She waits in the corner
With a warm smile
Calmly fighting my disease.

The noblest women I ever
Knew,
Pleasant, strong with humor,
Sly as night.

She is so earnest
In all her endeavors,
I shall hold her high
And sing her praises forever.

Molecules moving freely
Through space,
A change of form; a passing,
Transcending time and place.

One upon another
Constructing the cosmos,
The plurality of infinity,
The intermingling Eros.

For mind and matter are surely the sum,
Just as each of our planets were once one
Harmonizing our polarity and slowly
coming undone.

A mixture of anything in everything,
A piece of star, rock or even our son.

(For Anaxagoras, 500 B.C - 428 B.C.)

Goodbye old friend,
It is sad to go,
But I'm sure will meet again.

I'll be out on the border drifting
And when the wind blows
I want you to listen,
For in that gentle summer breeze
Is the kingdom and all its keys.

Roaming the supple countryside
Searching for food, seeking
Shelter from the cold.

In darkness I hide,
Covering my undesirable
Situation from the reserved world.

Walking slowly down
The state's long highway,
Leaving a life I knew
for the short days and long nights
to reveal the answers to questions I know.

Many have gone before,
Virtue, diligence, moderation
And charity is what
I was taught.

Thoughts in my head
Bounce along as they will,
Taking my time,
Getting my fill.
Time marches on
And I pause to reflect,
For I could be wrong.

Tears that float to
The icy water's edge,

Meeting the electrical
Currents from your altered
Earth.

Beginning a series,
A series of honorable quests
Under your sultry sun.

In the caves of immigration's dilution,
Somber soldier's lay down
Their guns
And engage in the causal
Conversation of home life.

Generals, retired, return to
Civilian life carrying
Out civic duties with didactic
Military precision.

Shadow ghosts visit us again,
Another turn on the smooth wheel of time,
Another heartbeat passes,
Breathe in, breathe out.

So many cycles for a night
To hold.
Fear aside, emotions of old
Creep in slowly from the
Long forgotten annals of mood.

Covered wagons pass
Slowly by,
Looking to recycle
The metal of yesterday's
Industry.
Mind or matter,
Ebb and flow,
Emotions and possessions
Come and go.

A single cell
Has taught me well.
Jumping in happiness,
Bursting in bliss,
I send you a hug
And await your kiss.

Your joy is overflowing,
Your color always glowing,
Never alone
Here at home.

You abound in love,
This I can tell,
You're a part of me
My single cell.

Reply:
"Simple. Made you smile.
That is all
For awhile."

(For Sasha ☺)

Across the pond,
Over the hill and down the road
Lives the life I used to know.

The odyssey has carried me away,
I wanted to stay,
But the wind blew
Hard and stole the day.

So new lives I make,
Each building toward
What was,
Each looking back and adding pieces for
Tomorrow's cause.

Arrow's flight
toward wood of time,
Wish they would move
But paradoxes proved,
Infinity never concludes.

(For Zeno, 490 B.C. - 430 B.C.)

The world is a mirror
And I am the glass
Reflecting the future
Built on the past/
Fortune moves forward
And heaven comes at last.

Animals cheer in blind
Excitement/
Flowers push through
Soft brown dirt
And blossom in sunlight
To heal our hurt.

A lifetime has passed/
Practicing magic for the spirit realm,
Watch in cautious wonder,
As God can overwhelm.

How sensitive our muses
Remain, how time has a feel
That can seem so strange.

I dreamt of my wife as I journeyed
To lands far away,
I longed for the day,
I'd hear you say,
The life of love
 Is the only way.

The legend tells us
Of four heroes passing winter
Roads in the mountains of
The illusioned and the unreal.

In reaches of my mind
I created a journey;
A quest for immortals,
A blessing from a king's seal,
For an uncounted number of years
I digitized
The bright pilgrimage,
How I have traveled so far
Home seems foreign.

All I have left is scripted instructions
Of what I must teach.
A man lives and is lucky with love.
With help from above,
Meaning has come.

We learn the way from elders they say,
Spend a day
Alone to pray.

Forgive me,
here I am bathed in
life-stained white,
confused and
determined
not to lose.

Bright with pelting rain,
Madness and instinct
Are going insane.
Care for me
As I am true,
Ask about me
And I'll come looking for you.

Balance two roads and you may win,
Metamorphically it makes sense to gather
So much and constantly
Condense,
To live in your head,
Wondering at the end of life
What will be said?

I read the epic tales of heroes, warriors
and goddesses
Meeting with fate in the dark evening
Hours.
Stories of morals, vices and celestial
consolations.

The fortune or foil of mingling
With deities, the lessons
The same in each ode of old,
Do no wrong and a fortune you will hold.

I captured your city
Square outside a small apartment window.
Looking across the bustling downtown
I recognized the awkward synchronization
Of your metropolitan flow.

Other buildings climbed the sky calling us
To look in several directions at once
As the people, small and distant,
 hustled to their
Appropriate places.

It was mid December
And I met you for the first time.
We talked all night and left our doubts
Behind.
I laughed for a while,
At shadow puppet's transverse line.

The clouds rolled back displaying
hand magic's lifeline bind,
Unweaving your strings to uncover a
Friendship that is benign.

The floor was met with crawling
Bodies searching for anonymous pleasure.
The air was depleted oxygen
And liquids of all kinds reigned supreme,
The huddled masses before your off color
Performers were the majority
Of the minority.

Amazed by the swaggering illusions of
your old blues man. Rookies and those
clouded with the pleasures of the night
were not able to see what was carefully
revealed.

Penalties are set in stone and the path is
narrow and hard to follow.
In the course of many seasons passage,
the careful eye found a way and set about
following your blues singer
whose saddest song was
silence.

Dancing in velvet shoes,
People pass and the
Jazz man sang the blues.

A change of course
In summers of song and verse.

The vibe was life,
The frequency
Set at drum and fife.

Set to your old ways,
Logically bound
And stubborn religious phase
Have pleasantly abstained.

Great men scourge the
Street begging for money,
Fighting to eat.

Disguised as paupers
Are the heroes of before,
Studying the night, hungry for more.

People we've known for
So many lives',
Careening along the corridors
Of competition's delight.

During the day my mind awoke
Slowly, progressively
Attuning to the vibrancy
And hidden energy frequencies
Surrounding the metropolitan flow
Of man, communal living systems,
I found synergies and sub-matrixes
Of complex fashions melting in the
wireless
Communications of mass
Networks of people's illusions.

Then the subtleties of life were added,
The grand delusion
Of grass playing complicated mind
Games with man
While contemplating the navigation of
ants.

People we meet,
Where do they go?
If you look about
Maybe you'll know,
They never really leave,
The possibilities
I try to conceive,
A change of form
And I begin to believe.

Shake me, exit this
Cold nightmare,
Release the songbird
Floating in air.
Bury me tomorrow, after a day
Of mourning; forgotten oaths
And simple transgressions
I heeded their warning.

All now past.
All now counted.

Come before us
The judges sit on high,
Languidly we pass,
Praying to fly.

Brass bands put down their instruments,
Now the music speaks in different ways,
Enter our women of multiplication's
jubilation.

To the East
We rode, coming
Down in steady
Droves,
New remnants
Of an ancient code,
Looking for fruit
The harvest never
Sold,
Waiting in wonder
And put on hold.
Construct miracles,
Then watch them explode.

I'll see you when the stars
All come out
To play.
When the sun is low
And the moon is
On its way.

This is when
A thousand heartbeats
Strain to be still,
To see the love
Of a women
And the strength
Of her will.

Peasants joined the careening wail of a
lost nation.
Studying the enclosures of lava flow
formation.
Whipping winds amongst the palm trees
creation,
If the sand wasn't a stone,
I'd shape it like a clam and call it my
home.

Now the tide has come again,
Rinsing the sand
to cleanse the land.

I called to you
And there you were,
To fill a thousand promises
And leave me wanting more.
An angel of angels
With a pleasant
Steady sound
I heard you
Whisper
It is love
You found.

In the steady rush of the cannonballs
Arch,
A distant
Cloud parted and rays of sunlight
Prepared for it's touch.
Remarkable voyage to the carpeted
Battlefield.
Ode to the heroes who walked straight
And tall into the mist,
Once again your service
Reminds us of what is not to be missed.
Seven trumpets from heaven
Did sound and solemnly announce
The mighty iron balls fall
And crash to the ground.

Trapped, the snare laid
In wait, hidden, obstructed in a remote
Corner.
Only beasts and wild men journey here.
There is no rest, no parting,
The ceaseless beating of the ocean
Lost upon those of the deep
Inland.
Replaced by the desire
And need to be in flux.
There is no rest, no respite.
I lay my heart on the coldest, smoothest
stone
Waiting for the vanquished to return
Soon I loathsomely join their ranks
And file past those who have no regard,
The intensity of the cool metal on my
Hands is replaced
By the saturation heat
Of an equinox sky.
Shuffling to the center
I declare I am fit
And look for respite
There is none.
They seek to whittle us,
Erode us into shoots and shadows of our
former selves,
A body conquered can never rest
But a mind that's free can fly through any
sky.

And so once again
Out on the edge,
I remain.
Whittling a sculpture
That will guide you and bring you comfort
When you pass through.
A humble figure
But one all the same,
A portrait of achievement,
A long forgotten name.
And so in the distance I hustle
Building stars that will carve a path,
A testament of my will
And a bright premonition for those who
Last.

In the emptiness
I paint with the tools I have
Collected on my journey there,
Soft brushes made of pine,
Warm colors made of brine,
A fragile imagination
Wish it was mine.
So who am I to decide,
How to fill this space,
I must turn back
And bring forth the human
Race.
In all your drama
And strife,
What is it that would capture
The glory that is life.

Walk along this abandoned river,
See the souls that once were,
Remember?
Look back into the frail recollections
Of the winter wind,
Surely the seasons can not take blame.
Certainly the clouds, the grass and the
people
Will not be guilty.

Now it is a little clearer.
This was abandoned for your sake,
So you can cultivate, reshape and remake,
Perform your magic,
Return and tell us your fate.

Circle of houses, neighborhoods,
Lined pavement,
Decadence swirls in fluorescence.
Commuters,
Tall building prominence.
Strangers and friends,
Cultural woven highway bookends.
Along upper canal districts,
Where water yields too reemerge,
Ideals surfaced and freelancers converge.
Reflective glass towers
And multiplicity of uphill struggles,
Summits bathed in the manila yellow
Of assimilated foreigners.
Transparent runs the bureaucracy
Too mellow to follow,
Researchers meet specimens
In the parks wooden hollow.
Combos of concrete grey and natural
green,
Lives the smiley face of my IM dreams,
Sending messages, real as they seem,
A disjointed life preened,
then flew away in urban essence extreme.

(For the City of Worcester, MA)

Fields and meadows, barking dogs.
Moon guards and planted mind hogs.
Forests that live in cities,
Creatures showing humans pity.
Abstract ideals selected,
Made a living as a dreamer defecting,
Open arms and steady extension
Will you join me in this dimension?

Planning for what may never come to be,
Lost in unraveling unbirthed reality,
Set to music and sold for free -
Take it away then give it back to me.

So what do these words mean
And are they what they seem,
What is not there
adds little to life,
Hold to the known
As thin as the air.

I died a million deaths
Each forged in splintered remembrance,
What was the brief undertaking of the
moment,
Who now carries the banner to its
fulfillment?
Where is this new place I have landed,
ascended, descended,
But certainly and swiftly reconfigured.
And when the light is dim and distant
And the hell hounds nip and chase at my
heels
I call to you;
Recounting our paternal oaths
And realize there is no moment without
meaning,
There is no passion without being.

So I settle like weight in the sand
And am awakened to life
In many instances, moments and
locations,
Pulsing with the stale breath
Of living after death.
I thank the originator and smile at Osiris,
Certainly leaving seems so sweet after
you arrive.

Arms outstretched
From the moment we met.
Lessons of your innocence
Kept in ritual and remembrance,
Tales of your immaculate conception
Keep us from a life of unholy
transgression.
Building a life to mirror your ways -
Your blessed Virgin
Worthy of praise.

Melting nerves,
Slow serious thought curves,
The mind wanes
And suddenly serves,
The higher order,
The greater
Good,
I wish I would
And know I should,
Pray all day
And completely
Obey.

What became of you
Who worked the fields
Night and day,
Through the seasons
And for no pay?

What became of you
Who drove me here,
With little to say
And an incredible fare?

And you who are near
What is your destiny in a future year?

All seasons came out to see
A girl, a ballgame,
And the chosen path of the free.

Drifting clouds dripping wet fuse,
A storm in the sky,
A paradigm set to comply,
A white buckled daydream
As a passing muse,
A return to a simpler time,
A fleeting rewind,
A mind vision for the blind.

Shallow holes we dig,
Constructing a means to an end,
A justified
Beginning
Will arise/two beings crossed in time.
Looking back how far
To journey?
A million miles more,
We lost no one along the way.
The shore is filled with friends
Waiting and robed in marble/
Rapt muted glory.
Where is your ideal in the wind?
Where does it rest in the element
penetration,
Take time to explore this new region
It is home and strange,
It remains and therefore retains
Our interest it entertains.
Look away and see the grass sway
Part the sea and be on your way.

About a story we all read,
Locomotive constitution
Slowly churning uphill,
Pumping and puffing,
Pulling uncounted weight.

Fantasy of the night,
Scribbled poet's lines
That the stars recite.

Steel rail,
Curving landscape,
Carrier of freight,
Deliverer of western pioneer supply,
Voyage for the ordinary.
Interwoven, intricate, infinite stories,
One long pilgrimage where all are present
and
Everything's extraordinary.

You told me a joke
In the strangest of seasons,
I held you for a moment
And you gathered your reasons.
I'll stand by you, straight and true,
I'll kindle our hearts and set you apart,
We'll make music our muse
And love our art.

Whistling drones, copper shards singing
In melodramatic, whining tones
Profuse, brunt electronics
Hemorrhaging refuse.

Gateways of rhythm,
Patented pathway sensation
Of a musical nation.

In back rooms where birth lives
cords of my stringed instrument,
Playing the part of mechanics gone mad,
Orchestra pit strumming techno type fad.

Music of machines
Wired sound of
Chips
going round and round.

Hacking firewalls
Of fantasies galaxies
where fury muses
in programmed nurseries.

Frayed speeding optic
Transformers meeting octave,

Steel nipples and the death of thought.

Pass Age
Beckoning beat
drama and melody
summer heat
distant drum dance
pounding feet
enter the circle
jump the fire
tested by flame
melted or tamed
the outcomes the same

A long cast shadow.
Are you reaching for light?
Do you aim for total darkness?
Are you hiding?
In your shaded contours
We still see lines and shapes
And outlines of objects.
You must love the discrete,
Or has it been forced on you?
Would you rather come out
To where we will know
The intimate details of
Objects in your path.
How long have you remained
In darkened lines of obscurity?
Does your image orbit with solar
reliability?
Are you left in some dark corner
Awaiting a rearrangement?
Are you intune
With a universal shadow,
Coaching you in your half dark state.
How are you used by others?
Are you satisfied to be
An image in half
Shading what others might see.

Slanted, jagged and cutting,
It rips through the landscape
Encasing cattle ranchers
Of surveyed plots of franchisement.

Like abandoned avenues
It stretches to the horizon
And meets the fiery sun
That shines down on it so authoritatively.

I race my hand across
The sharp steel
Knowing my sustenance is safe
And cut myself only to watch the blood
drip into the dust.

Oort cloud, nebular egg-womb
Of the unbound, drifting, drifting
Hardly found.

Swirling, whirling, curling and twirling,
Density compacted before the unfurling.
Every opposite races in harmony,
Every creation has its own tree.

Mind visions, existence, exploration
And sub-particle fissions.

Spirit dances throughout thought pattern
commotion,
Dust, aggregate, seed sprout formation.
Birth pain, explosion, symmetry
Fitting into place, scattered space.

But have we moved an inch,
Or are we still entrenched,
Everything and anything
The size of a single salt pinch?

Mind composite matter, tangible electrical
neurons
Of molecular splatter.

Lunar colors, is every particle connected
in multi-verse fetus expansion,
or so my mind-atom wonders.

In simple times there was a bride,
Glory to me for she was all mine.
In troubled times she stood by my side
And for eternities turn I shall be forever
kind.
In her is my morning star and in me her
evening tea,
Beside each other we shall be -
in good times, bad times and all those in
between.

Jackstraws, standing tall
In the warmest days
Bending slightly
As the breezes say,
See my balmy golden stalk,
Take in the breadth
Of my supple supply.
Seed of seven for years of plenty,
Silos of slender stock shadows
For years of slight.
Evens and odds or devils and gods,
I serve the fields
And sacrifice my fronds.

Traffic, avalanche,
Polluted rivers
Steady stream,
Release me from these
Maddening dreams.

Floating, snarled crag,
Frightened children remembered.
A sound that startles the night watchmen,
Melody beer cure.

Slow, dried
Fruit hangs from the longhouse's
pine rafters,
Hunting skins, meat
And procurement.

Had enough of exploding seed stuff,
Give me game of the frail and for the
tough.

Away and afar,
The hills gave way to the mountains.

Aviators, flying V formation, logical
sense to symmetries
Sensation,
Faster, warmth is receding,
Rest for rejuvenation after migrations
season.
Perennial spot, fixed in minds navigator,
Returned to a dot
Among an endless equator.

A ring of flame, circled stone
Dancing in moonlight's wane,
A clover of cards, premonitions façade,
Do you believe in garlic clothed bards?

But she dances like moving fish swim,
Dresses swaying without any pins,
Circling the wagons and wondering if
Her voice is a deadly siren sin?

Tarots for nickels and crystals for bills,
Longing to look deep in her green-eyed
skill,
Romanian trails and monkeys on sticks,
Hard luck begat her mysterious tricks.

The future is calling and the picture is
clear, two souls captive in a mystery held
dear, a million moons more for my gypsy
and I to adore.

Parlor dances, frying pan eggs, warm
milk. Little distractions, cool bursts of
breeze, open window, sunlight in and out,
clouds. AM, talk about transportation,
memories, one about a summer dress,
another to call a friend. Electricity noise,
inadequate lighting, the 50s, a rolling
black car, outdoor noise, coming together,
swaying in the rhythm of solitude.

On a dresser, photographs, the past,
timelines captured, printed, displayed,
fresh cotton, neatly folded, on one side,
wrinkled on the other. A mirror, oval,
gold plated border, peeling crosshair
wallpaper, brown/yellow wall stain,
audible clock, the tea is ready, nightgown
on the floor, returning.

It is our image, two is one, one is two, that
is love, birth, history, childhood and age;
caretakers. Returning to a place once
familiar, a necklace, running errands, not
wanting to leave in the storm, carry it
always, I'll be there, will you come too, a
secret place, known to everyone.

To request copies, comment
or contact the author
please email:
penumbra0101@yahoo.com

www.ingramcontent.com/pod-product-compliance
Lightning Source LLC
Chambersburg PA
CBHW070530030426
42337CB00016B/2173